EFC 2024 Adventure Book - The hands-on book for the European Football Championship

LogikLichter

Hello and welcome to the biggest football festival of the year - Euro 2024! With this book, you won't just be watching, you'll be right in the thick of it and become part of the exciting European Football Championship yourself.

"EM 2024 Adventure Book - The Join-in Book for the European Football Championship for Children" is your perfect companion to experience the tournament. You'll discover something new on every page of this book and can even write down your own thoughts and results about the matches.

Your journey starts with an exploration of the great football stadiums in Germany, where the best teams from all over Europe compete against each other. You will learn more about the teams and can record the results on your own match schedule.

After each match day, there are exciting questions that you can answer. This allows you to make your own thoughts about the games and record what you particularly liked or what surprised you.

There are also cool puzzles and fun football facts every day to show you just how exciting football can be. From tricky word puzzles to exciting quizzes - there's something new to discover and learn every day.

Are you ready to start your European Championship? Then grab a pen, open the first page and get started.

Your own EFC adventure is waiting for you!

Contents

Olympiastadion Berlin

Von Rebecca Leisten www.rebecca-leisten.de - Eigenes Werk, CC BY-SA 4.0,
https://commons.wikimedia.org/w/index.php?curid=51963059

The Olympiastadion in Berlin, with a capacity of 70,033 spectators, is a place rich in history and great football moments. Built for the 1936 Olympic Games, this stadium hosted the 2006 World Cup final. The home club is Hertha BSC, and the stadium is considered one of the most important sporting arenas in Germany.

Stadiums

Stadium Dortmund

Von Arne Müseler / www.arne-mueseler.com, CC BY-SA 3.0 de,
https://commons.wikimedia.org/w/index.php?curid=85465522

Borussia Dortmund's home ground offers space for 61,524 international visitors. Famous for the "Yellow Wall", the largest standing-room-only stand in Europe, the stadium has been a symbol of passionate football and an impressive atmosphere since its opening in 1974.

Düsseldorf Arena

Von Peter Weihs - https://www.duesseldorf-tourismus.de/attraktionen/merkur-spiel-arena-6e20c61937, CC BY-SA 4.0, https://commons.wikimedia.org/w/index.php?curid=126483192

The home arena of Fortuna Düsseldorf has a capacity of 46,264 spectators. Opened in 2005, this stadium is the smallest at EURO 2024, but impresses with its modern design and a closable roof that offers a wide range of event options.

Stadiums

Waldstadion Frankfurt

Von Arne Müseler / www.arne-mueseler.com, CC BY-SA 3.0 de,
https://commons.wikimedia.org/w/index.php?curid=116955604

Frankfurt am Main is home to the Waldstadion, the home of Eintracht Frankfurt, with a capacity of 48,057 spectators. Originally built in 1925, the stadium has a rich history, including hosting European Championship and World Cup matches.

Stadiums

Auf-Schalke-Arena

Von Walter Koch - Eigenes Werk, CC BY-SA 4.0, https://commons.wikimedia.org/w/index.php?curid=77363679

The Auf-Schalke-Arena in Gelsenkirchen, the home of Schalke 04, can accommodate 49,471 spectators. Opened in 2001, it is known for its retractable roof and football pitch, making it one of the most modern arenas in Europe.

9

Stadiums

Volksparkstadion Hamburg

The Volksparkstadion in Hamburg, the home of Hamburger SV, is an impressive arena with a capacity for 50,215 spectators. Opened in 1953, the stadium underwent extensive modernisation in 1998. It has already hosted matches at the 1988 European Championships and the 1974 and 2006 World Cups.

Stadiums

Stadium Köln

Von © Raimond Spekking / CC BY-SA 4.0 (via Wikimedia Commons), CC BY-SA 4.0,
https://commons.wikimedia.org/w/index.php?curid=89386644

With a capacity of around 46,000 spectators, the Cologne stadium is one of the smaller stadiums at Euro 2024. It was built especially for the 2006 World Cup and has been the venue for the DFB Women's Cup final since 2010.

Stadiums

Stadium Leipzig

The stadium in Leipzig, with a capacity of 46,635 spectators, is an impressive example of modern stadium architecture, built within the historic walls of the old central stadium. As the home ground of RB Leipzig, the arena combines the historical significance of the old stadium with innovative construction methods.

Stadiums

Football Arena München

Von Richard Bartz, Munich aka Makro Freak - Eigenes Werk, CC BY-SA 2.5,
https://commons.wikimedia.org/w/index.php?curid=3687540

With a capacity of 66,026, the Arena in Munich, home of FC Bayern Munich, is one of the most modern football arenas in the world. Known for its impressive, colour-changing façade, it is a real eye-catcher and symbol of progressive stadium architecture.

Stadiums

Arena Stuttgart

Von Arne Müseler / www.arne-mueseler.com, CC BY-SA 3.0 de,
https://commons.wikimedia.org/w/index.php?curid=118286652

The arena in Stuttgart, which can accommodate 50,998 spectators, is the home of VfB Stuttgart. Originally built in 1933, the stadium was extensively modernised for the 2006 World Cup and combines historical significance with modern comfort.

Group A

Germany

Scotland

Hungary

Switzerland

Group A

Germany, as three-time European champions, will face Scotland, Hungary and Switzerland. Scotland and Hungary have shown consistency with multiple appearances, but have had limited success. Switzerland, a regular participant, is looking for a breakthrough beyond the round of 16.

17

Groups

Group B

Spain

Croatia

Italy

Albania

Groups

Group B

Spain, three-time European champions, will compete with Croatia, Italy and Albania. Croatia, always a strong competitor, and Italy, European champions in 1968, are established teams. Albania, with limited European Championship experience, will be hoping for a surprise.

Group C

Slovenia

Denmark

Serbia

England

20

Group C

Slovenia, Denmark, Serbia and England meet in this group. Denmark, European champions in 1992, and England, semi-finalists, are the favourites. However, Slovenia and Serbia, with less European Championship experience, could spring a surprise.

Groups

Group D

Winner Play Off A

Netherlands

Austria

France

Groups

Group D

This group combines the play-off A winner with the Netherlands, Austria and France. The Netherlands, European champions in 1988, and France, two-time European champions, are the prominent teams, while Austria will be looking for more than preliminary round success.

Group E

Belgium

Slovakia

Romania

Winner Play Off B

Groups

Group E

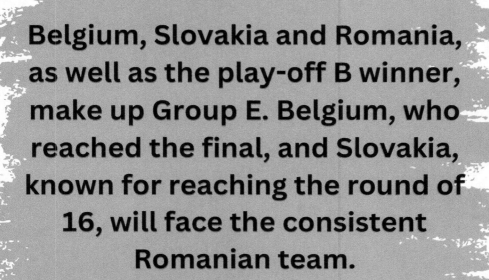

Belgium, Slovakia and Romania, as well as the play-off B winner, make up Group E. Belgium, who reached the final, and Slovakia, known for reaching the round of 16, will face the consistent Romanian team.

Groups

Group F

Turkey

Winner Play Off C

Portugal

Czech Republic

26

Groups

Group F

Turkey, Portugal, the Playoff C winner and the Czech Republic are in Group F. Portugal, European champions in 2016, and the Czech Republic, European champions in 1976 (as Czechoslovakia), are the standout teams, while Turkey will be hoping for a strong finish.

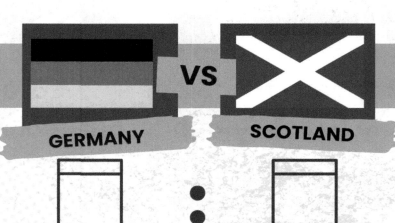

VS

GERMANY   **SCOTLAND**

:

Fr, 14.06.2024 – 21:00
Group A, München

28

GAME DAY 1
14.06.

WHERE AND WITH WHOM DID YOU WATCH THE GAME?

_____
_____
_____

WHAT WAS THE DECISIVE SCENE IN THE GAME AND WHY?

_____
_____
_____
_____

RECORD OF THE DAY

With 53 games, Germany has played the most European Championship matches. That's a whole lot of football!

QUIZ OF THE DAY
SCORE THE GOAL!

GROUP STAGE
GAME DAY 1
SATURDAY 15.06.2024

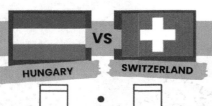

HUNGARY **VS** **SWITZERLAND**

:

Sa, 15.06.2024 – 15:00
Group A, Köln

SPAIN **VS** **CROATIA**

:

Sa, 15.06.2024 – 18:00
Group B, Berlin

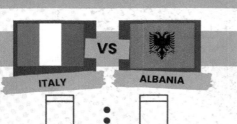

ITALY **VS** **ALBANIA**

:

Sa, 15.06.2024 – 21:00
Group B, Dortmund

32

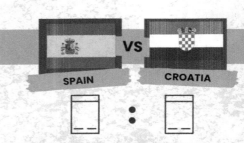

GAME DAY 1
15.06.

WHERE AND WITH WHOM DID YOU WATCH THE GAME(S)?

_____
_____
_____
_____

WHICH PLAYER STOOD OUT TO YOU IN PARTICULAR AND WHY?

_____
_____
_____
_____

RECORD OF THE DAY

Do you know Kacper Kozłowski? He became the youngest player at a European Championship at 17 years and 246 days!

15.06.
QUIZ OF THE DAY
FIND THE FOOTBALL TERMS

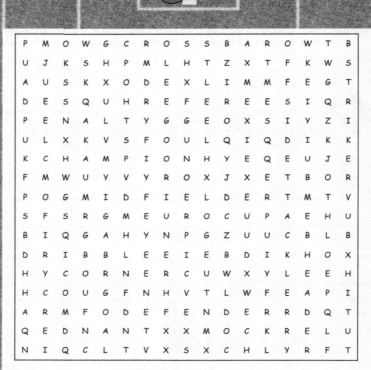

P	M	O	W	G	C	R	O	S	S	B	A	R	O	W	T	B
U	J	K	S	H	P	M	L	H	T	Z	X	T	F	K	W	S
A	U	S	K	X	O	D	E	X	L	I	M	M	F	E	G	T
D	E	S	Q	U	H	R	E	F	E	R	E	E	S	I	Q	R
P	E	N	A	L	T	Y	G	G	E	O	X	S	I	Y	Z	I
U	L	X	K	V	S	F	O	U	L	Q	I	Q	D	I	K	K
K	C	H	A	M	P	I	O	N	H	Y	E	Q	E	U	J	E
F	M	W	U	Y	V	Y	R	O	X	J	X	E	T	B	O	R
P	O	G	M	I	D	F	I	E	L	D	E	R	T	M	T	V
S	F	S	R	G	M	E	U	R	O	C	U	P	A	E	H	U
B	I	Q	G	A	H	Y	N	P	G	Z	U	U	C	B	L	B
D	R	I	B	B	L	E	E	I	E	B	D	I	K	H	O	X
H	Y	C	O	R	N	E	R	C	U	W	X	Y	L	E	E	H
H	C	O	U	G	F	N	H	V	T	L	W	F	E	A	P	I
A	R	M	F	O	D	E	F	E	N	D	E	R	R	D	Q	T
Q	E	D	N	A	N	T	X	X	M	O	C	K	R	E	L	U
N	I	Q	C	L	T	V	X	S	X	C	H	L	Y	R	F	T

1. GOAL
2. PENALTY
3. CORNER
4. OFFSIDE
5. REFEREE
6. MIDFIELDER
7. STRIKER
8. DEFENDER
9. DRIBBLE
10. HEADER
11. TACKLE
12. FOUL
13. CROSSBAR
14. EUROCUP
15. CHAMPION

GROUP STAGE
GAME DAY 1
SUNDAY 16.06.2024

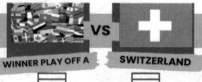

WINNER PLAY OFF A VS **SWITZERLAND**

	:	

Su, 16.06.2024 – 15:00
Group D, Hamburg

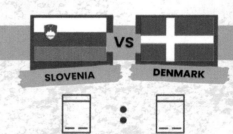

SLOVENIA VS **DENMARK**

	:	

Su, 16.06.2024 – 18:00
Group C, Stuttgart

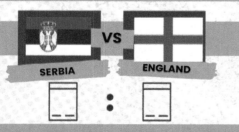

SERBIA VS **ENGLAND**

	:	

Su, 16.06.2024 – 21:00
Group C, Gelsenkirchen

36

WHERE AND WITH WHOM DID YOU WATCH THE GAME(S)?

_____

_____

_____

IMAGINE YOU ARE A COMMENTATOR: HOW WOULD YOU DESCRIBE THE MOST EXCITING MATCH OF THE DAY?

_____

_____

_____

_____

RECORD OF THE DAY

Gábor Király, the goalkeeper from Hungary, holds the record as the oldest player at a European Championship - he was 40 years and 86 days old.

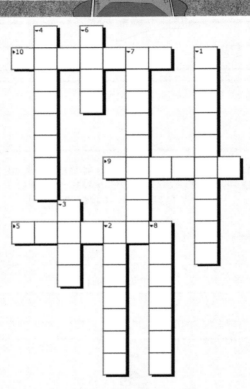

1. This player guards the goal.
2. The game starts with this.
3. Another term for a tie in a match.
4. A player who plays in front of the goalkeeper.
5. A player responsible for scoring goals.
6. The main equipment used in football.
7. The line surrounding the playing field.
8. The official who enforces the rules of the game.
9. The number of players in a football team (excluding substitutes).
10. A shot at goal, often awarded for fouls.

GROUP STAGE
GAME DAY 1
MONDAY 17.06.2024

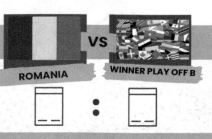

ROMANIA VS **WINNER PLAY OFF B**

☐ : ☐

Mo, 17.06.2024 – 15:00
Group E, München

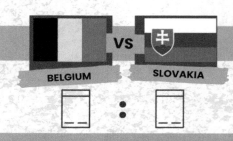

BELGIUM VS **SLOVAKIA**

☐ : ☐

Mo, 17.06.2024 – 18:00
Group E, Frankfurt

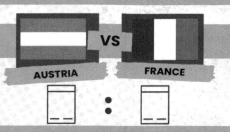

AUSTRIA VS **FRANCE**

☐ : ☐

Mo, 17.06.2024 – 21:00
Group D, Düsseldorf

GAME DAY 1
17.06.

WHERE AND WITH WHOM DID YOU WATCH THE GAME(S)?

WHO SCORED YOUR PERSONAL GOAL OF THE DAY?

RECORD OF THE DAY

In Euro 2004, Wayne Rooney became England's youngest ever goal scorer in the tournament at the age of 18.

17.06.
QUIZ OF THE DAY
GUESS THE FLAGS!

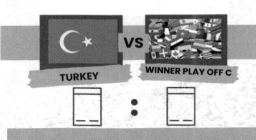

TURKEY VS **WINNER PLAY OFF C**

:

Tu, 18.06.2024 – 18:00
Group F, Dortmund

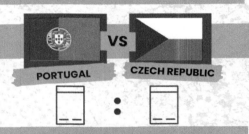

PORTUGAL VS **CZECH REPUBLIC**

:

Tu, 18.06.2024 – 21:00
Group F, Leipzig

GAME DAY 1
18.06.

WHERE AND WITH WHOM DID YOU WATCH THE GAME(S)?

_____
_____
_____

WHICH TEAM HAD THE BETTER STRATEGY AND WHAT WOULD YOU DO DIFFERENTLY AS A COACH?

_____
_____
_____
_____

RECORD OF THE DAY

Germany has won the most European Championship matches with a total of 27.

18.06.
QUIZ OF THE DAY
WHICH PLAYER WILL SCORE THE GOAL?

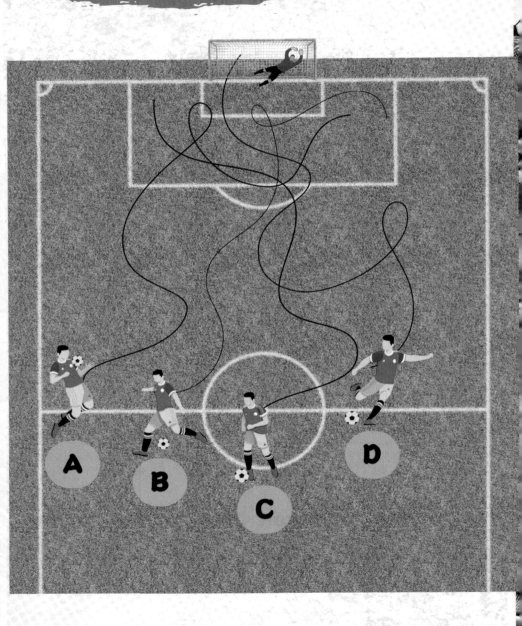

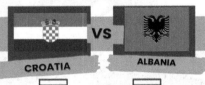

CROATIA   VS   **ALBANIA**

__ : __

We, 19.06.2024 – 15:00
Group B, Hamburg

VS

GERMANY   **HUNGARY**

__ : __

We, 19.06.2024 – 18:00
Group A, Stuttgart

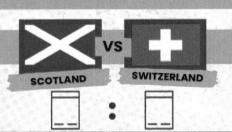

SCOTLAND   VS   **SWITZERLAND**

__ : __

We, 19.06.2024 – 21:00
Group A, Köln

GAME DAY 2
19.06.

WHERE AND WITH WHOM DID YOU WATCH THE GAME(S)?

_____
_____
_____

WAS THERE A RESULT OR A GAME SITUATION THAT WAS COMPLETELY DIFFERENT TO WHAT YOU EXPECTED?

_____
_____
_____
_____

RECORD OF THE DAY

The highest victory at a European Championship was 6:1 - the Netherlands against Yugoslavia in 2000.

49

GROUP STAGE
GAME DAY 2
THURSDAY 20.06.2024

SLOVENIA VS **SERBIA**

☐ : ☐

Th, 20.06.2024 – 15:00
Group C, München

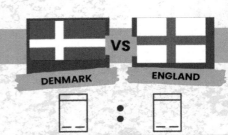

DENMARK VS **ENGLAND**

☐ : ☐

Th, 20.06.2024 – 18:00
Group C, Frankfurt

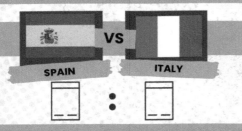

SPAIN VS **ITALY**

☐ : ☐

Th, 20.06.2024 – 21:00
Group B, Gelsenkirchen

GAME DAY 2
20.06.

WHERE AND WITH WHOM DID YOU WATCH THE GAME(S)?

_____
_____
_____

WHAT WAS YOUR PERSONAL HIGHLIGHT OF THE DAY, APART FROM THE GOALS AND MOVES?

_____
_____
_____
_____

RECORD OF THE DAY

During Euro 2020, England's captain, Harry Kane, was one of the top goal scorers of the tournament.

20.06.
QUIZ OF THE DAY
FIND THE FOOTBALL TERMS

```
N V S H H H Y V N Y X K N Y D E K
H I F J M G O A L P O S T U R Q A
Y N V F G U Q Z F M Y P S J B R T
E J A Y S T A D I U M D Q M A V R
L U V Y E X T R A T I M E L T I R
L R X W E W A Y H D O T W Q Q D S
O Y Q H O L Q W I N G E R Y U T W
W T I N N Y W S G A R F M A H W
C I S S C C R J L K I U P I L R Q
A M N T P U F R E E K I C K I O Z
R E L L Q O U L N U V H Y C F W I
D H S E I X J W V P H N F Z I I M
N F O R M A T I O N Y B X J E N J
J F L O F F S I D E T R A P R V W
Y K E E P E R P X H T X T O S F K
E S P J S U B S T I T U T I O N N
J K S K T R O P H Y O X B W J T D
```

1	Keeper	2	ThrowIn	3	Whistle
4	Substitution	5	OffsideTrap	6	Winger
7	FreeKick	8	Goalpost	9	Formation
10	YellowCard	11	ExtraTime	12	InjuryTime
13	Stadium	14	Qualifiers	15	Trophy

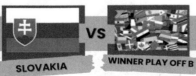

SLOVAKIA VS **WINNER PLAY OFF B**

:

Fr, 21.06.2024 – 15:00
Group E, Düsseldorf

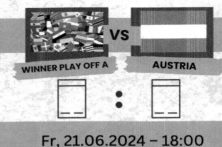

WINNER PLAY OFF A VS **AUSTRIA**

:

Fr, 21.06.2024 – 18:00
Group D, Berlin

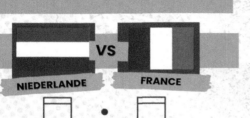

NIEDERLANDE VS **FRANCE**

:

Fr, 21.06.2024 – 21:00
Group D, Leipzig

56

GAME DAY 2
21.06.

WHERE AND WITH WHOM DID YOU WATCH THE GAME(S)?

_____
_____
_____

WHO DO YOU THINK WAS THE MOST CREATIVE PLAYER ON THE PITCH?

_____
_____
_____
_____

RECORD OF THE DAY

There were 11 own goals at the 2021 European Championship, more than in all previous tournaments combined.

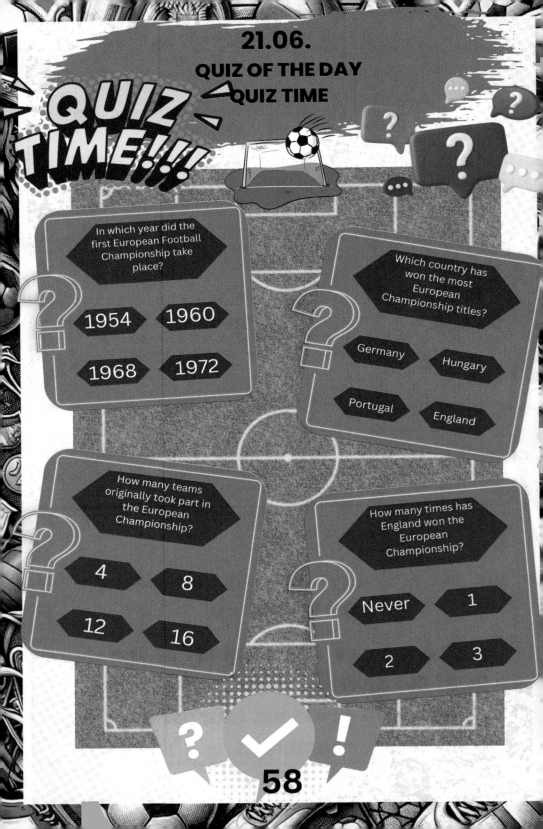

GROUP STAGE
GAME DAY 2
SATURDAY 22.06.2024

 VS

WINNER PLAY OFF C   **CZECH REPUBLIC**

Sa, 22.06.2024 – 15:00
Group F, Hamburg

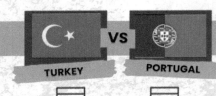

TURKEY   **PORTUGAL**

Sa, 22.06.2024 – 18:00
Group F, Dortmund

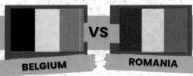 **VS**

BELGIUM   **ROMANIA**

Sa, 22.06.2024 – 21:00
Group E, Köln

60

GAME DAY 2
22.06.

WHERE AND WITH WHOM DID YOU WATCH THE GAME(S)?

_____
_____
_____

WHAT PREDICTIONS FOR THE GAME WERE COMPLETELY UPENDED?

_____
_____
_____
_____

RECORD OF THE DAY

Cristiano Ronaldo is the first player to score in 5 different European Championship tournaments: he scored in 2004, 2008, 2012, 2016 and 2021.

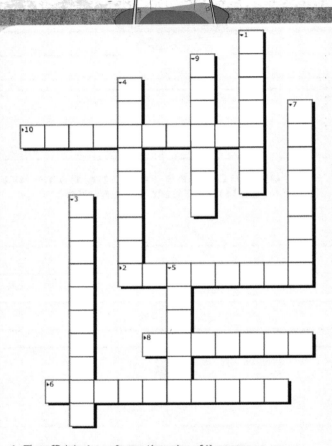

1. The official who enforces the rules of the game.
2. A method used to restart play after the ball has gone out over the goal line.
3. The player who can use their hands within the box.
4. A technique used to control or move the ball.
5. A pass from a teammate that leads directly to a goal.
6. A rectangular area where the goal is located.
7. When a player scores three goals in a single game.
8. A temporary suspension of play.
9. The act of propelling the ball with your head.
10. A player known for their ability to control and pass the ball.

VS

SWITZERLAND   **GERMANY**

:

Su, 23.06.2024 – 21:00
Group A, Frankfurt

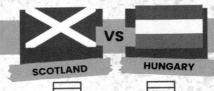

VS

SCOTLAND   **HUNGARY**

:

Su, 23.06.2024 – 21:00
Group A, Stuttgart

GAME DAY 3
23.06.

WHERE AND WITH WHOM DID YOU WATCH THE GAME(S)?

_____

_____

_____

HOW DID YOU FEEL WHEN THE GAME STARTED AND HOW DID THAT CHANGE BY THE END?

_____

_____

_____

_____

RECORD OF THE DAY

Switzerland needed 8 games for their first victory at a European Championship.

23.06.
QUIZ OF THE DAY
SCORE THE GOAL!

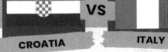

CROATIA VS **ITALY**

Mo, 24.06.2024 – 21:00
Group B, Leipzig

ALBANIA VS **SPAIN**

Mo, 24.06.2024 – 21:00
Group B, Düsseldorf

GAME DAY 2
24.06.

WHERE AND WITH WHOM DID YOU WATCH THE GAME(S)?

_____

_____

_____

WHICH TEAM EXCEEDED YOUR EXPECTATIONS AND WHICH DISAPPOINTED?

_____

_____

_____

_____

RECORD OF THE DAY

Spain had the most consecutive games without conceding a goal (7 games between 2012 and 2016).

GROUP STAGE
GAME DAY 3
TUESDAY 25.06.2024

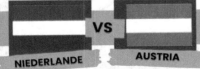 VS

NIEDERLANDE **AUSTRIA**

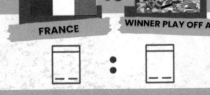 VS

FRANCE **WINNER PLAY OFF A**

☐ **:** ☐

☐ **:** ☐

Tu, 25.06.2024 – 18:00
Group D, Berlin

Tu, 25.06.2024 – 18:00
Group D, Dortmund

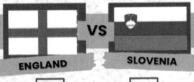 VS

ENGLAND **SLOVENIA**

 VS

DENMARK **SERBIA**

☐ **:** ☐

☐ **:** ☐

Tu, 25.06.2024 – 21:00
Group C, Köln

72

Tu, 25.06.2024 – 21:00
Group C, München

WHICH GAME(S) DID YOU WATCH AND WITH WHOM?

_____

_____

_____

WHICH TEAM HAD THE BETTER STRATEGY AND WHAT WOULD YOU DO DIFFERENTLY AS A COACH?

_____

_____

_____

_____

RECORD OF THE DAY

England reached the finals for the first time in 2020, finishing as runners-up.

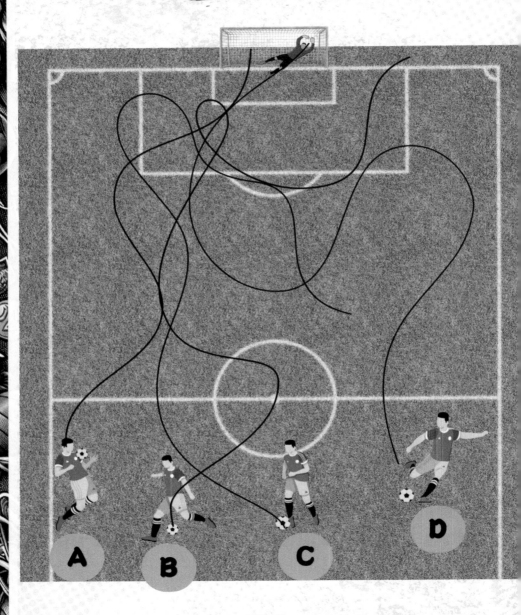

GROUP STAGE
GAME DAY 3
WEDNESDAY 26.06.2024

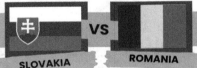

SLOVAKIA VS **ROMANIA**

We, 26.06.2024 – 18:00
Group E, Frankfurt

WINNER PLAY OFF B VS **BELGIUM**

We, 26.06.2024 – 18:00
Group E, Stuttgart

CZECH REPUBLIC VS **TURKEY**

We, 26.06.2024 – 21:00
Group F, Hamburg

WINNER PLAY OFF C VS **PORTUGAL**

We, 26.06.2024 – 21:00
Group F, Gelsenkirchen

GAME DAY 2
26.06.

WHERE AND WITH WHOM DID YOU WATCH THE GAME(S)?

_____
_____
_____

WHO DO YOU THINK WAS THE MOST CREATIVE PLAYER ON THE PITCH?

_____
_____
_____
_____

RECORD OF THE DAY

England's first appearance in the UEFA European Championship was in 1968.

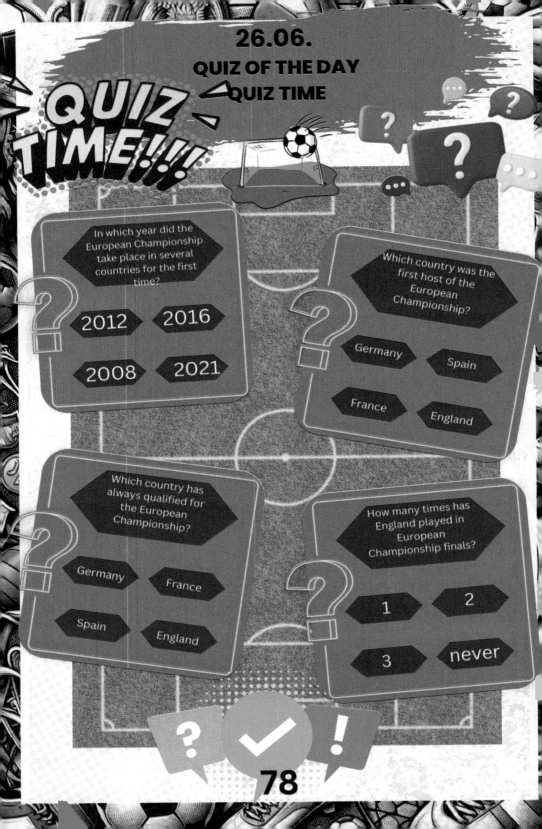

FINAL SCORE
GROUP STAGE

Group A

Standing	Goals	Points
1.		
2.		
3.		
4.		

Group B

Standing	Goals	Points
1.		
2.		
3.		
4.		

Group C

Standing	Goals	Points
1.		
2.		
3.		
4.		

Group D

Standing	Goals	Points
1.		
2.		
3.		
4.		

Group E

Standing	Goals	Points
1.		
2.		
3.		
4.		

Group F

Standing	Goals	Points
1.		
2.		
3.		
4.		

ROUND OF SIXTEEN

SATURDAY 29.06.2024

Second Gr. A **VS** Second Gr. B

Sa, 29.06.2024 – 18:00
Berlin

Winner Gr. A **VS** Second Gr. C

Sa, 29.06.2024 – 21:00
Dortmund

ROUND OF SIXTEEN
29.06.

WHERE AND WITH WHOM DID YOU WATCH THE GAME(S)?

_____

_____

_____

WHICH DRIBBLES OR INDIVIDUAL ACTIONS WERE PARTICULARLY EFFECTIVE?

_____

_____

_____

_____

RECORD OF THE DAY

Jogi Löw, the German national coach, was the first coach to be sent off at a European Championship.

QUIZ OF THE DAY
FIND THE FOOTBALL TERMS

```
N  U  T  X  S  F  W  I  I  K  D  X  J  J  C  H  N
W  Y  J  C  A  P  T  A  I  N  B  A  N  D  H  O  B
M  H  O  V  D  I  I  W  C  S  S  G  H  P  H  F  P
C  O  D  D  D  M  H  O  H  W  C  R  S  L  V  F  I
O  E  C  O  O  X  A  N  F  G  O  T  I  A  G  S  D
A  F  C  R  L  J  T  P  A  R  R  M  B  Y  U  I  V
W  W  O  B  V  G  T  K  N  O  E  N  E  O  C  D  G
P  P  R  B  V  S  R  E  Z  U  D  U  N  F  G  E  R
U  X  N  D  Z  D  I  G  O  P  P  E  C  F  O  L  M
D  A  E  K  V  C  C  N  N  S  N  O  H  S  A  I  K
W  S  R  G  A  L  K  U  E  T  C  T  S  O  L  N  D
Q  S  F  D  R  E  H  T  B  A  P  A  S  S  L  E  T
N  I  L  D  H  A  W  M  H  G  V  H  U  Y  I  G  P
I  S  A  S  C  T  O  E  S  E  U  Q  X  A  N  T  V
U  T  G  E  Z  S  L  G  G  S  G  J  K  O  E  K  K
J  J  Q  W  B  M  U  I  N  L  A  R  M  Q  O  Y  G
C  Y  K  H  E  I  B  M  I  E  Y  W  H  J  L  N  E
```

1. Assist
2. Pass
3. Nutmeg
4. Cleats
5. CornerFlag
6. OffsideLine
7. Score
8. Bench
9. CaptainBand
10. GroupStage
11. FanZone
12. HatTrick
13. GoalLine
14. Playoffs
15. VAR

ROUND OF SIXTEEN
SUNDAY 30.06.2024

Winner Gr. C **VS** Third D/E/F

☐ : ☐

Su, 30.06.2024 – 18:00
Gelsenkirchen

Winner Gr. B **VS** Third A/D/E/F

☐ : ☐

Su, 30.06.2024 – 21:00
Köln

ROUND OF SIXTEEN
30.06.

WHERE AND WITH WHOM DID YOU WATCH THE GAME(S)?

_____
_____
_____

WERE THERE ANY FUNNY OR UNEXPECTED EVENTS DURING THE GAME?

_____
_____
_____

RECORD OF THE DAY

Lothar Matthäus has the longest gap between his first and last European Championship appearance: 20 years and 6 days.

Second Gr. D **VS** Second Gr. E

 :

Mo, 01.07.2024 – 18:00
Düsseldorf

Winner Gr. F **VS** Third A/B/C

 :

Mo, 01.07.2024 – 21:00
Frankfurt

WHERE AND WITH WHOM DID YOU WATCH THE GAME(S)?

_____

_____

_____

WHAT ROLE DID SET PIECES (CORNERS, FREE KICKS) PLAY IN TODAY'S GAME?

_____

_____

_____

_____

RECORD OF THE DAY

Luke Shaw, England, scored the fastest goal in a European Championship final in 2021 after just 1:56 minutes.

ROUND OF SIXTEEN
TUESDAY 02.07.2024

Winner Gr. E **VS** Third A/B/C/D

☐ : ☐

Tu, 02.07.2024 – 18:00
München

Winner Gr. D **VS** Second Gr. F

☐ : ☐

Tu, 02.07.2024 – 21:00
Leipzig

WHERE AND WITH WHOM DID YOU WATCH THE GAME(S)?

_____
_____
_____

HOW DID THE TEAMS REACT TO THE SUBSTITUTIONS? WAS THERE A NOTICEABLE CHANGE IN THE GAME?

_____
_____
_____
_____

RECORD OF THE DAY

Italy have not conceded a goal in 22 European Championship matches so far.

QUARTER FINALS

FRIDAY 05.07.2024

Winner ROS 3 **VS** Winner ROS 1

:

Fr, 05.07.2024 – 18:00
Stuttgart

Winner ROS 5 **VS** Winner ROS 6

:

Fr, 05.07.2024 – 21:00
Hamburg

QUARTER FINALS
05.07.

WHERE AND WITH WHOM DID YOU WATCH THE GAME(S)?

WHO DO YOU THINK WAS THE MOST CREATIVE PLAYER ON THE PITCH?

RECORD OF THE DAY

Denmark has the most defeats at the European Championship with 17 games.

101

QUARTER FINALS

SATURDAY 06.07.2024

Winner ROS 4 **VS** Winner ROS 2

 :

Sa, 06.07.2024 – 18:00
Düsseldorf

Winner ROS 7 **VS** Winner ROS 8

Sa, 06.07.2024 – 21:00
Berlin

WHERE AND WITH WHOM DID YOU WATCH THE GAME(S)?

_____

_____

_____

WHAT FORMATION DID THE WINNING TEAM USE AND HOW DID THIS CONTRIBUTE TO THEIR SUCCESS?

_____

_____

_____

_____

RECORD OF THE DAY

England failed to win their opening game the most times (5 draws, 4 defeats).

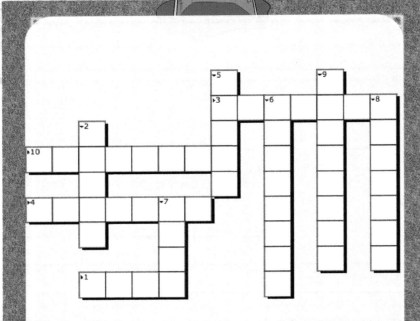

1. A score in football.
2. The surface on which the game is played.
3. A card shown for severe rule violations.
4. The start or resumption of play.
5. A high ball sent across the field or into the penalty area.
6. A player primarily responsible for stopping opposing attacks.
7. A rule violation; often results in a free kick.
8. A quick move to get past an opponent.
9. A formal break during the game.
10. Protective gear worn on the legs of players.

SEMI FINALS

TUESDAY 09.07.2024

Winner QF 1 **VS** Winner QF 2

:

Tu, 09.07.2024 – 21:00
München

WHERE AND WITH WHOM DID YOU WATCH THE GAME?

_____
_____
_____

WHAT TACTICAL CHANGES HAVE YOU NOTICED FROM THE COACHES?

_____
_____
_____
_____

RECORD OF THE DAY

Renato Sanches became the youngest European champion at the age of 18 years and 11 months.

SEMI FINALS

WEDNESDAY 10.07.2024

Winner QF 3 **VS** Winner QF 4

We, 10.07.2024 – 21:00
Dortmund

110

WHERE AND WITH WHOM DID YOU WATCH THE GAME?

_____

_____

_____

WERE THERE ANY PARTICULAR PHYSICAL PERFORMANCES, SUCH AS SPRINTS OR JUMPING POWER, THAT STOOD OUT TO YOU?

_____

_____

_____

_____

RECORD OF THE DAY

The song "Three Lions" became an iconic anthem for England during Euro 1996 and has remained a popular football song in England.

10.07.
QUIZ OF THE DAY
FIND THE FOOTBALL TERMS

```
I  B  W  P  S  P  A  M  M  W  A  L  L  P  M  T  A
F  Q  U  L  L  P  W  G  I  P  T  C  V  H  T  X  F
N  B  R  A  C  E  J  D  D  T  C  R  O  S  S  B  F
T  F  X  Z  V  R  D  E  F  F  S  C  N  J  C  N  T
F  L  I  C  K  O  N  F  I  W  L  E  A  G  U  E  A
D  C  P  I  D  O  K  E  E  C  P  I  B  T  S  G  C
Y  P  L  L  K  I  T  N  L  X  M  P  S  D  E  E  T
M  F  X  C  C  W  M  D  D  M  G  M  S  U  J  D  I
V  Y  D  T  X  D  A  E  R  Y  M  O  A  N  U  F  C
B  Z  G  B  Y  B  A  G  F  T  D  J  E  E  E  O  I
U  F  Q  D  K  K  G  O  J  P  S  Q  B  R  N  R  U
I  R  Y  V  V  G  E  Q  C  B  T  K  R  D  M  W  H
M  A  T  O  S  P  R  S  U  B  S  C  X  O  Q  A  D
M  C  O  M  E  B  A  C  K  J  O  K  P  G  L  R  W
T  U  M  R  L  Q  L  G  L  S  X  P  C  U  G  D  M
E  G  T  I  S  T  K  E  Q  T  U  P  I  H  C  N  E
```

1. Manager
2. Cross
3. Save
4. Kit
5. League
6. Defender
7. Forward
8. Midfield
9. Brace
10. Tactic
11. Subs
12. Wall
13. FlickOn
14. Underdog
15. Comeback

112

FINALE

SUNDAY 14.07.2024

Winner SF 1 **VS** Winner SF 2

:

Su, 14.07.2024 – 21:00
Berlin

FINALE
14.07.

WHERE AND WITH WHOM DID YOU WATCH THE GAME?

_____
_____
_____

HOW DID YOU FEEL WHEN THE GAME STARTED AND HOW DID THAT CHANGE BY THE END?

_____
_____
_____
_____

RECORD OF THE DAY

At 36 years and 331 days, Giorgio Chiellini was the oldest captain of a European champion.

CHAMPIONS

SOLUTIONS

14.06.
QUIZ OF THE DAY
SCORE THE GOAL

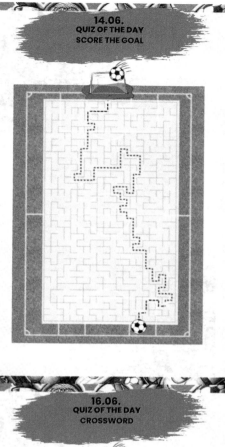

15.06.
QUIZ OF THE DAY
FIND THE FOOTBALL TERMS

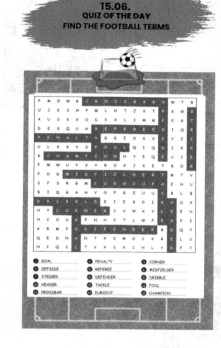

1. GOAL
2. OFFSIDE
3. STRIKER
4. HEADER
5. CROSSBAR
6. PENALTY
7. REFEREE
8. DEFENDER
9. TACKLE
10. EUROCUP
11. CORNER
12. MIDFIELDER
13. DRIBBLE
14. FOUL
15. CHAMPION

16.06.
QUIZ OF THE DAY
CROSSWORD

17.06.
QUIZ OF THE DAY
GUESS THE FLAGS

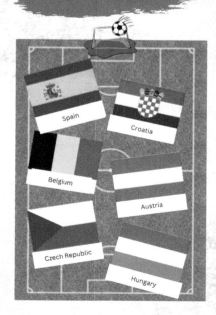

18.06.
QUIZ OF THE DAY
WHO SCORES THE GOAL?

19.06.
QUIZ OF THE DAY
GUESS IT RIGHT!

How many countries have taken part in the European Football Championship at least once since it began? (55)

How many spectators can the largest stadium ever to host a European Championship match hold? (81.000, Wembley)

How many goals were scored in total at the 2016 European Championship? (108)

How many balls were officially used at Euro 2016? (800)

20.06.
QUIZ OF THE DAY
FIND THE FOOTBALL TERMS

1. Keeper
2. Substitution
3. FreeKick
4. YellowCard
5. Stadium
6. ThrowIn
7. OffsideTrap
8. Goalpost
9. ExtraTime
10. Qualifiers
11. Whistle
12. Winger
13. Formation
14. InjuryTime
15. Trophy

21.06.
QUIZ OF THE DAY
QUIZ TIME!

In which year did the first European Football Championship take place?
1960

Which country has won the most European Championship titles?
Germany

How many teams originally took part in the European Championship?
4

How many times has England won the European Championship?
Never

120

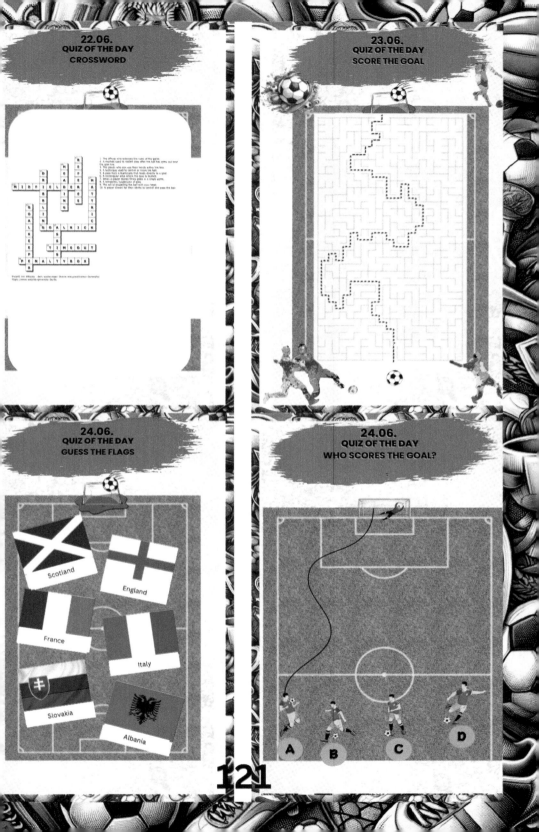

Scotland

England

France

Italy

Slovakia

Albania

A   B   C   D

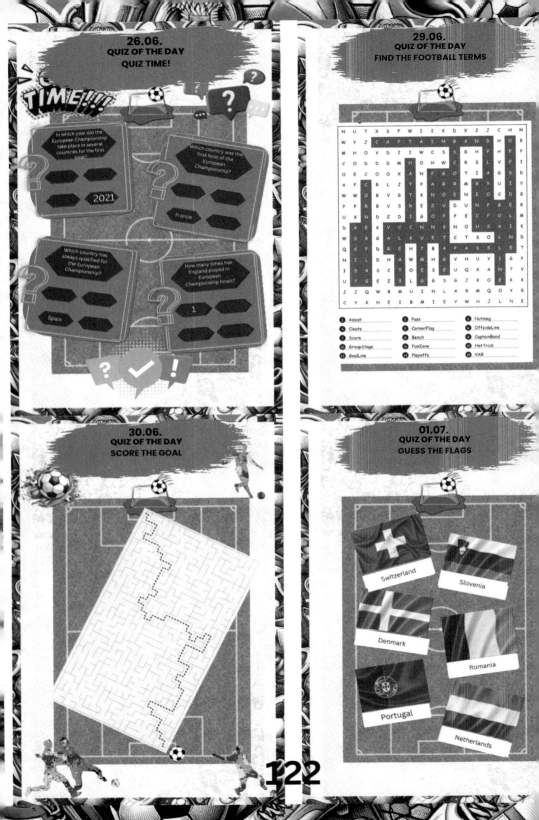

26.06.
QUIZ OF THE DAY
QUIZ TIME!

TIME!!!!

In which year did the European Championship take place in several countries for the first time?

2021

Which country was the first host of the European Championship?

France

Which country has always qualified for the European Championship?

Spain

How many times has England played in European Championship finals?

1

29.06.
QUIZ OF THE DAY
FIND THE FOOTBALL TERMS

N	U	T	X	S	F	W	I	I	K	D	X	J	J	C	H	N
W	Y	J	C	A	P	T	A	I	N	B	A	N	D	H	O	I
M	H	O	V	D	I	I	W	C	S	S	G	H	P	H	U	I
C	O	D	D	D	M	X	O	H	W	C	R	S	L	V	G	O
O	E	C	O	O	X	A	N	F	G	O	T	I	A	G	S	U
A	F	C	R	L	J	T	P	A	R	R	M	B	Y	U	A	I
W	W	O	B	V	G	T	K	N	O	E	N	E	O	C	D	I
P	P	R	B	V	S	R	E	Z	I	G	P	P	C	F	O	L
U	X	N	D	Z	D	I	G	O	P	D	U	N	F	G	E	I
A	E	K	V	C	C	N	N	S	M	P	E	C	F	O	L	M
D	W	S	R	G	A	L	K	U	E	T	C	T	S	O	L	N
Q	S	F	D	R	E	H	T	B	A	P	A	S	S	L	E	I
N	I	L	D	H	A	W	M	H	G	V	H	U	Y	I	G	I
I	S	A	S	C	T	O	E	S	E	U	Q	X	A	N	T	V
U	T	G	E	Z	S	L	G	G	S	G	J	K	O	E	K	K
J	J	Q	W	B	M	U	I	N	L	A	R	M	Q	O	Y	G
C	Y	K	H	E	I	B	M	I	E	Y	W	H	J	L	N	E

1. Assist
2. Pass
3. Nutmeg
4. Cleats
5. CornerFlag
6. OffsideLine
7. Score
8. Bench
9. CaptainBand
10. GroupStage
11. FanZone
12. HatTrick
13. GoalLine
14. Playoffs
15. VAR

30.06.
QUIZ OF THE DAY
SCORE THE GOAL

01.07.
QUIZ OF THE DAY
GUESS THE FLAGS

Switzerland

Slovenia

Denmark

Romania

Portugal

Netherlands

02.07.
QUIZ OF THE DAY
WHO SCORES THE GOAL?

05.07.
QUIZ OF THE DAY
WHO SCORES THE GOAL?

How many games without conceding a goal did Italy play at European Championships? **22**

Which country has participated in the most European Championships? **Germany**

Who is the youngest player ever to have taken part in a European Championship? **Kozłowski**

How many draws did England achieve at European Championships until 2021? **18**

06.07.
QUIZ OF THE DAY
CROSSWORD

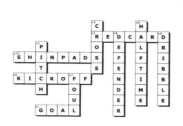

Crossword answers:
- C O N S... (2 down)
- R E D C A R D (3 across)
- P I T C H (2 down)
- S H I N P A D S (10 across)
- K I C K O F F (4 across)
- G O A L (1 across)
- H A L F T I M E (9 down)
- D R I B B L E (8 down)
- F O U L (7 down)
- D E F E N D E R (6 down)

1. A score in football.
2. The surface on which the game is played.
3. A card shown for severe rule violations.
4. The start or resumption of play.
5. A high ball sent across the field or into the penalty area.
6. A player primarily responsible for stopping opposing attacks.
7. A rule violation; often results in a free kick.
8. A quick move to get past an opponent.
9. A formal break during the game.
10. Protective gear worn on the legs of players.

09.07.
QUIZ OF THE DAY
CROSSWORD

How often is a player fouled on average per game? (1-3)

How many headers does a player take on average per game? (8-10)

How many touches of the ball does a midfielder have on average per game? (70-100)

How many kilometres does a midfielder run on average per game? (12)

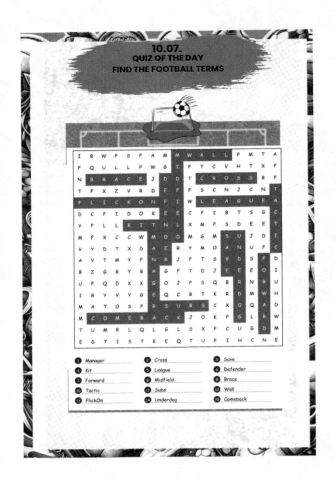

10.07.
QUIZ OF THE DAY
FIND THE FOOTBALL TERMS

I	B	W	P	S	P	A	M	M	W	A	L	L	P	M	T	A
F	Q	U	L	L	P	W	G	I	P	T	C	V	H	T	X	F
N	B	R	A	C	E	J	D	D	T	C	R	O	S	S	B	F
T	F	X	Z	V	R	D	F	F	S	C	N	J	C	N	T	
F	L	I	C	K	O	N	F	I	W	L	E	A	G	U	E	A
D	C	P	I	D	O	K	E	E	C	P	I	B	T	S	G	C
Y	P	L	L	K	I	T	N	L	X	M	P	S	D	E	E	T
M	F	X	C	C	W	M	D	D	M	G	M	S	U	J	D	I
V	Y	D	T	X	A	E	R	Y	M	O	A	N	U	F	C	
A	V	T	M	Y	F	N	R	J	F	T	S	V	D	S	F	D
B	Z	G	B	Y	B	A	G	F	T	D	J	E	E	E	O	I
U	F	Q	D	K	K	G	O	J	P	S	Q	B	R	N	R	U
I	R	Y	V	V	G	E	Q	C	B	T	K	R	D	M	W	H
M	A	T	O	S	P	R	S	U	B	S	C	X	O	Q	A	B
M	C	O	M	E	B	A	C	K	J	O	K	P	G	L	R	W
T	U	M	R	L	Q	L	G	L	S	X	P	C	U	G	B	M
E	G	T	I	S	T	K	E	Q	T	U	P	I	H	C	N	E

1. Manager _____ 2. Cross _____ 3. Save _____
4. Kit _____ 5. League _____ 6. Defender _____
7. Forward _____ 8. Midfield _____ 9. Brace _____
10. Tactic _____ 11. Subs _____ 12. Wall _____
13. FlickOn _____ 14. Underdog _____ 15. Comeback _____

Impressum:

LogikLichter Publishing is
represented by
Anton Wasilew
Erich-Zeigner-Allee 60a
04229 Leipzig
Germany
logiklichtergmail.com

Printed in Great Britain
by Amazon

39934576R00069